LMS
TURBINE LOCOMOTIVE
6202

R. S. CARTER

PETER WATTS
Publishing

ISBN 0 906025 08 7

Copyright 1979 Russell Carter

Published in Great Britain By
Peter Watts, Hill View, Fox Elms, Gloucester

Printed by Washington Printing, Cheltenham
First printing August, 1979

*[Left] 6202 leaves Mossley Hill
with an up Merseyside Express
[Eric Treacy]*

*[Front Cover] The 5.25 pm
Liverpool—Euston Express storms through
Wavertree with 6202 at the head
[Eric Treacy]*

*[Back Cover] From the
archives of G.E.C. Traction Ltd*

On familiar ground, 6202 passes Edge Hill on an up Merseyside Express [Eric Treacy]

L.M.S. TURBOMOTIVE NO. 6202
NON-CONDENSING TURBINE LOCOMOTIVE

It was in June 1935 that the L.M.S. put into service an express passenger locomotive, the design of which was a radical departure from the conventional recipricating engine.

In the years prior to this, great efforts had been made in design to improve the thermal efficiency, reliability, and greater availability of the steam locomotive, and it had been considered by some of the major designers of steam locomotives that the steam turbine offered an attractive way of attaining these ends.

Thus, under the direction of William Stanier, it was thought practical, whilst embodying the general mechanical design parameters of the "Princess Royal" type, to employ a turbine as a prime mover. So No. 6202 appeared ex-Crewe works, similar in appearance to the Princess Class but without the familiar cylinders and side rods, these being substituted by a non-condensing turbine,

triple reduction gear and flexible drive to the forward coupled driving wheels.

It was in 1932 that the Ljungstrom Company of Sweden had put into service a 2-8-0 non-condensing turbine locomotive based on an existing standard, the drive from a front-mounted turbine being through triple reduction gearing, and a jack-shaft final drive to the coupled wheels.

The operational trials of the loco showed considerable improvement on previous designs; it was simple and no great difficulty was evidenced on maintenance.

Due to this promising behaviour, and the known interest of the C.M.E. of the L.M.S., representatives of the railway and Metro-Vick were invited to Sweden to inspect the locomotive in operation, and having witnessed various trials a favourable impression was formed of its performance.

Thus, through the direction of Sir William Stanier, as he was later to become, and based on the report of the visit by his engineers, he asked Metro-Vick and the Ljungstrom Co. to collaborate with him in preparing a design for a 4-6-2 express passenger locomotive, to work in conjunction with the new Pacific type "Princess Royal" class locomotives then being built for the Euston-Glasgow run.

On these runs trains of 500 tons or more would be worked between the two cities, and after the required calculations were made it was decided that a turbine of at least 2000 hp would be required—non-condensing with steam at 250 p.s.i. and a temperature of 750°F, which Metro-Vick, with their practical knowledge on larger turbo-generators, undertook to manufacture for the L.M.S.

The forward turbine was bolted to the left-hand main frame, ahead of the leading coupled wheels, whilst the reverse turbine was bolted to the right-hand main frame. The former had sixteen stages, and the internal arrangement of the blading ensured the maintenance. of high efficiency over a wide speed range. The turbine shaft was directly connected to the high speed gear pinion, flexibility of drive between these units, being maintained by an intermediate hollow quill shaft fitted with a pair of flexible diaphram couplings. (See page 6, items 1,3&5.)

The reverse turbine, smaller and less powerful than the forward unit, consisted of four blades only, and drove, through an additional single reduction gear, the high speed pinion. This unit was normally out of mesh with the main gear system, but when engaged had an overall ratio of 77:1. It was engaged by means of a sliding splined shaft and dog clutch which was originally operated by steam. This method however, caused a major failure in service, and was modified to hand-operation. In order to ensure that the teeth of the two parts of the clutch engaged correctly, not opposite each other, a ratchet inching mechanism was fitted. (See items 2,4&5 on page 6).

Steam from the boiler was admitted to the forward turbine by operating a normally positioned regulator lever in the cab via the steam-chest, formed as a steel casting containing six control valves. These were operated by a hand wheel in a clockwise direction in sequence from the cab, being situated in the position normally occupied by the reversing screw (L. H. of cab).

For the reverse turbine steam was admitted to a steam-chest containing three control valves. A interlocking mechanism prevented the reverse turbine clutch from being engaged until the handle was in the neutral position with all valves closed. The reverse turbine valves could not be opened until the reversing clutch was properly engaged, and similarly the ahead turbine valves could not be opened when the reverse turbine was connected to the gear train. A second inter-lock prevented any movement of the handle to engage the reverse turbine clutch unless the locomotive was stationary.

The turbine pinion formed the basis of the double helical triple reduction gear to the leading coupled axle. With an overall ratio of 34.4 to 1, the whole gear train was enclosed in a fabricated gear case, suspended from three supports on the locomotive frame, also being restrained from sideways movement.

In a reciprocating locomotive the differential movement between frame and wheel/axle-boxes is freely permitted by the use of connecting and coupling rods as a driving medium. However in a turbine locomotive where a gear system drive is employed within the frames, this relative movement must be catered for by a different method, and this was resolved by arranging that the final wheel assembly surrounded the driving axle, and was coupled to it by a series of floating pins and carrying links.

The final gear wheel assembly, which ran in white metalled bearings rigidly attached to the gear case enclosing the whole train, consisted essentially of three main parts; a gear rim (slow speed) and left and right hand centre discs bolted together to form one unit, which was free to move radially within the gear rim. Power was transmitted from the gear rim to the centre discs through a series of laminated springs arranged circumferentially round the wheel. These relieved the teeth from shocks which would otherwise be directly transmitted to there from the wheels.

The lubrication of the turbines was of the utmost importance, and after modifications to the original system, a three-pump closed circuit force feed layout was found to be the most effective and efficient. Each pump drew oil from a sump integral with the gear-case, and passed it under pressure, to all the bearings and through sprayers on to the gear teeth.

One pump, at the rear of the gear-case was reversible and was driven by the final gear through a small step-up gear, and only worked when the locomotive was moving. The other two were steam-driven reciprocating types which supplemented the mechanical

Official photographs showing 6202 ex Crewe Works in June, 1935 [National Railway Museum]

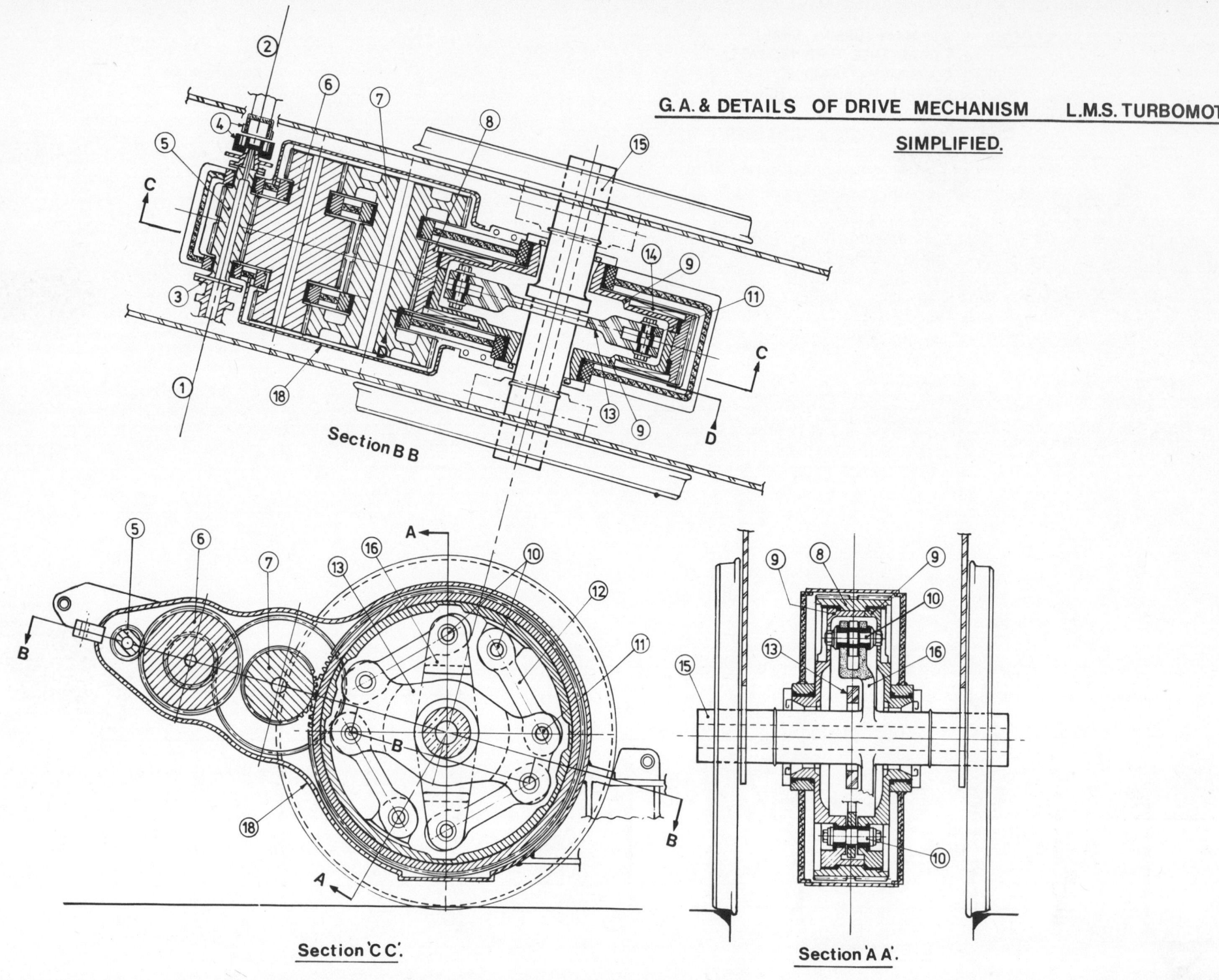

G.A. & DETAILS OF DRIVE MECHANISM   L.M.S. TURBOMOTIV

SIMPLIFIED.

Section B B

Section 'C C'.

Section 'A A'.

6

LEGEND.
1. ℄ OF MAIN TURBINE SHAFT.
2. ℄ OF REVERSE TURBINE SHAFT.
3. DIAPHRAGM COUPLINGS.
4. REVERSE TURBINE CLUTCH.
5. TURBINE PINION.
6. 1" INTERMEDIATE SHAFT & GEAR.
7. 2" " " " "
8. RIM GEAR. (SLOW SPEED.)
9. L.H. & R.H. CENTRE DISCS.
10. DRIVE PINS (4).
11. FLOATING PINS (4).
12. CARRYING LINKS.
13. FLOATING LINK.
14. LAMINATED SPRINGS.
15. DRIVING AXLE.
16. DRIVING ARM.
17. BEARINGS THUS ▬.
18. GEAR CASE.

FOLLOW THROUGH OF FORWARD GEAR DRIVE.
ITEMS 1 TO 3 5 6 7 8 THRO 14 TO 9 THRO.
10 TO 12 THENCE THRO.11 TO 13 THRO.10 TO
16 AND 15 THENCE TO DRIVING WHEEL.

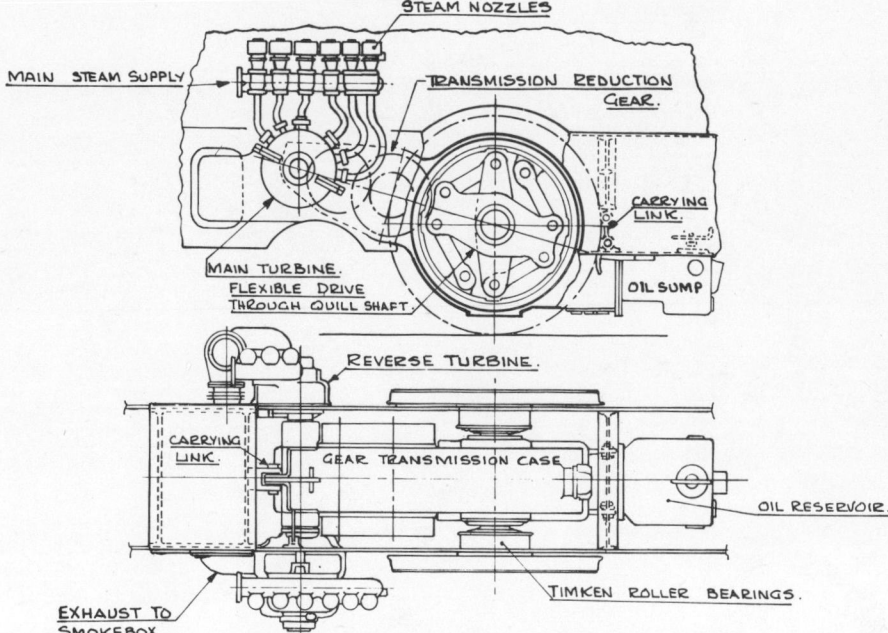

General Arrangement of Drive.

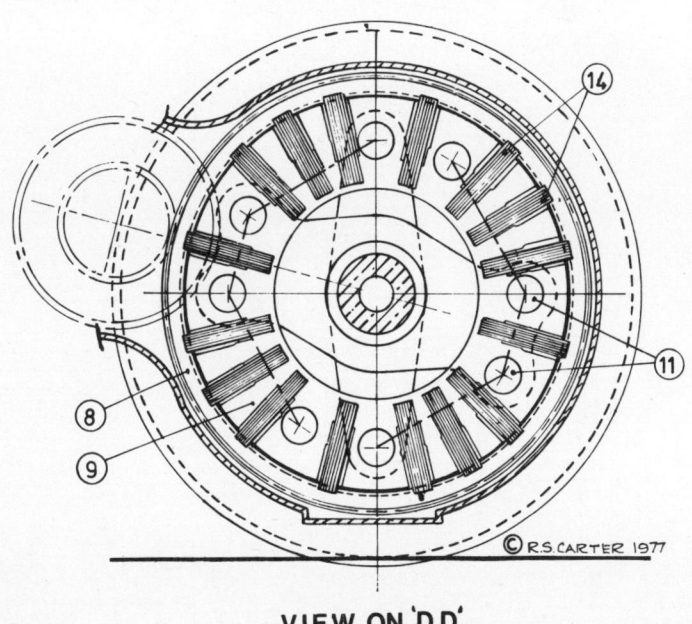

© R.S. CARTER 1977

VIEW ON 'DD'.

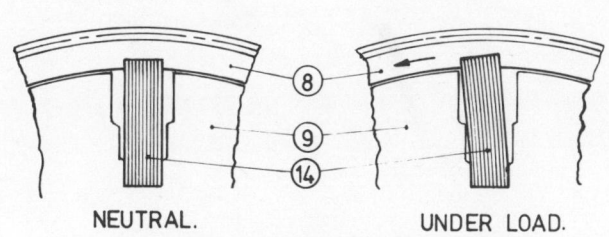

NEUTRAL.   UNDER LOAD.
OPERATION OF LAMINATED SPRINGS.

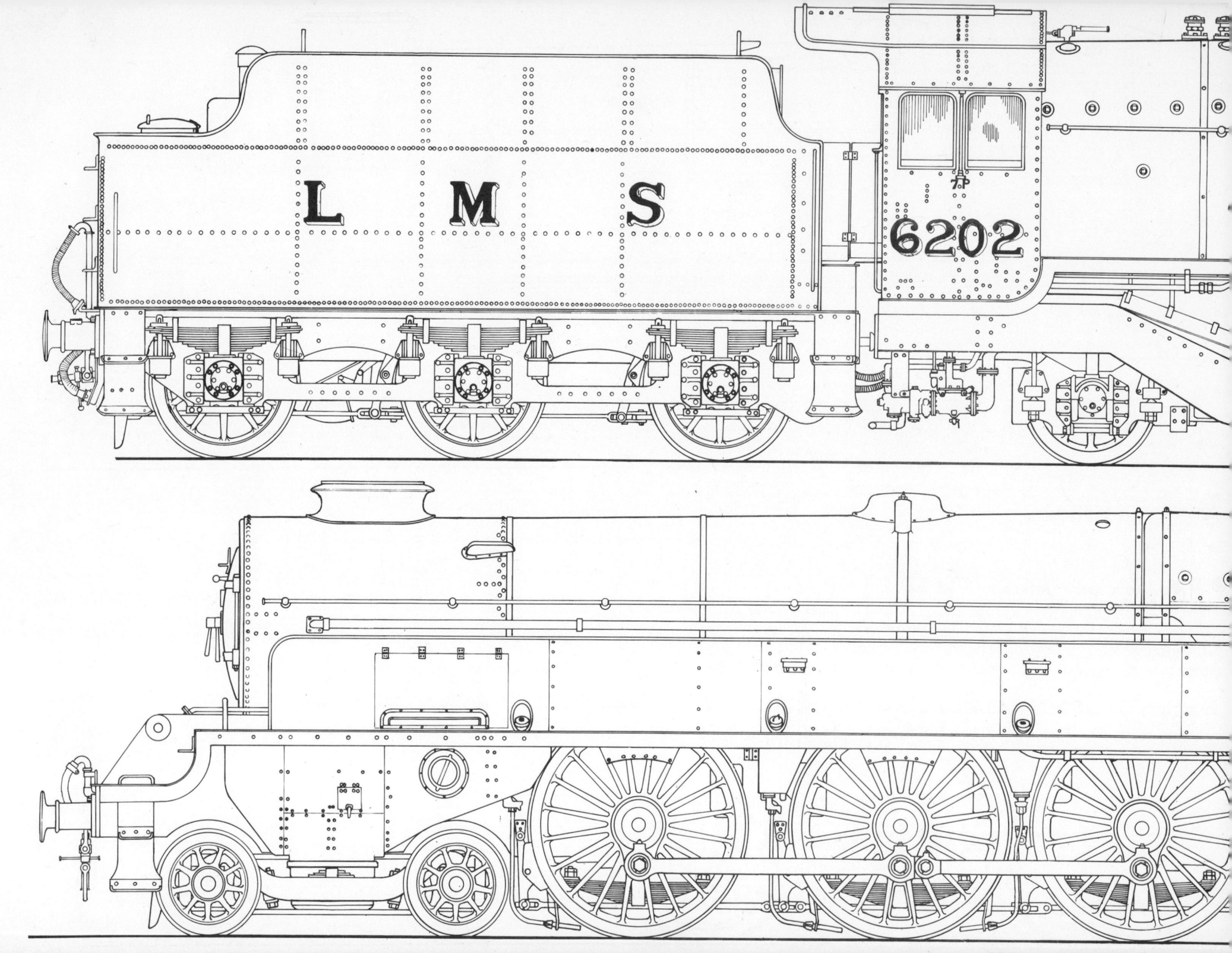

LMS 6202

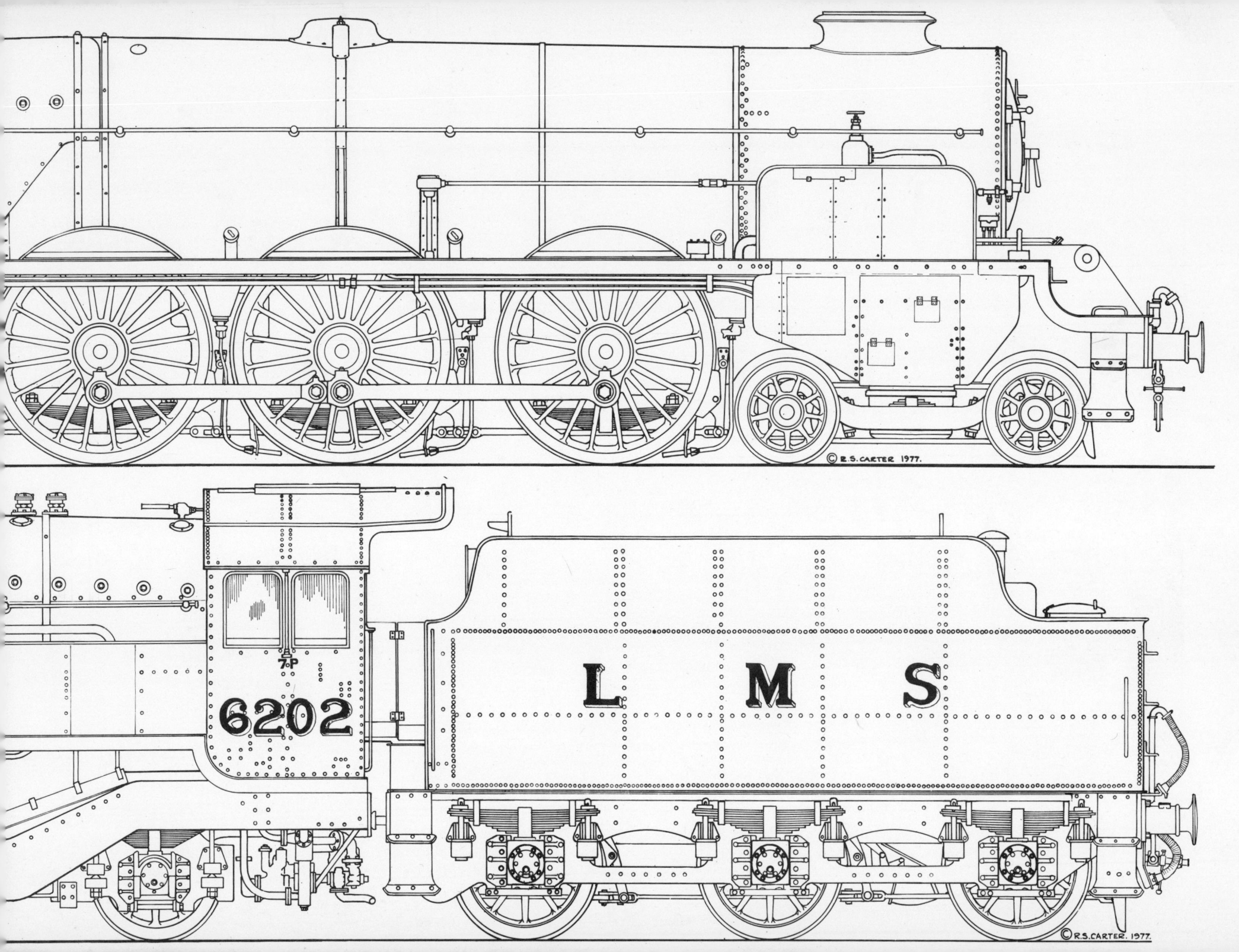

Three-quarters relative position drawing from the archives of G.E.C. Traction Ltd.

6202 during July 1936, having been fitted with new boiler and 40 element superheater [National Railway Museum]

pump supply, and were kept working all the time the locomotive was stationary in order to carry away heat along the turbine shaft to the journals. The feeds of all three pumps combined and passed through an air radiator—type cooler situated between frames immediately below the smoke-box.

The pressure from the two steam-pumps was approximately 7lbs/sq. in. and the gear pumps increased this pressure in the main circuit to 16lbs/sq. in., both pressures being indicated in the cab, as well as the temperature of the oil before entering (150°F) and leaving (90°F) the cooler.

The general mechanical design of the locomotive, which embodied the turbine and gear-case described above, followed the lines of the Princess Class locomotives, being built at the same time, there being one difference—all axles were fitted with roller-bearing axleboxes which over the years in service were never replaced.

From the time 6202 entered service it was employed almost entirely on the Euston—Liverpool run, except for some experimental tests with the dynamometer car between Euston and Glasgow to compare the performance with that of the ''Princess Royal'' Pacifics.

In the first ten years of operation, in spite of problems inherent in an experimental type, and a period between October 1939 and July 1941 when withdrawn from traffic, 6202 covered 400,000 miles. During that time there were major breakdowns of a serious nature which can be summarised as follows:- Six due to failure of the reverse

turbine, four to oil leakage, and one, the most serious, a failure in the flexible drive between the slow speed gear-wheel and the leading couple axle.

Failures with the turbines could cause a very disconcerting situation both to the locomotive and to the dislocation of traffic, since it meant that the wheels were locked and the locomotive could not be moved until the leading drivers were jacked up and the side rods removed. Inspite of the set-backs and the consequent expensive and time-consuming repairs, which meant long periods out of traffic, the work done by this experimental locomotive showed up in an increasingly favourable light over the years with a view to perhaps building a batch of locomotives incorporating the lessons learnt. However, in the changed circumstances of locomotive operation in the early 1950's, and the heavy expenses involved in re-newing the main turbine, it was decided to rebuild the engine as a standard 4 cylinder ''Pacific''.

Thus, in June 1952, 6202 emerged from Crewe works as B.R. 46202 ''Princess Anne'', in appearance a cross between a ''Princess Royal'' and a ''Duchess''. Nevertheless a handsome-looking locomotive.

Sadly its career was short, for on 8th October 1952, B.R. 46202 was involved in the horrific double collision at Harrow and Wealdstone Station, and was so badly damaged that it was withdrawn and eventually scrapped—a sorry end to a praiseworthy locomotive experiment.

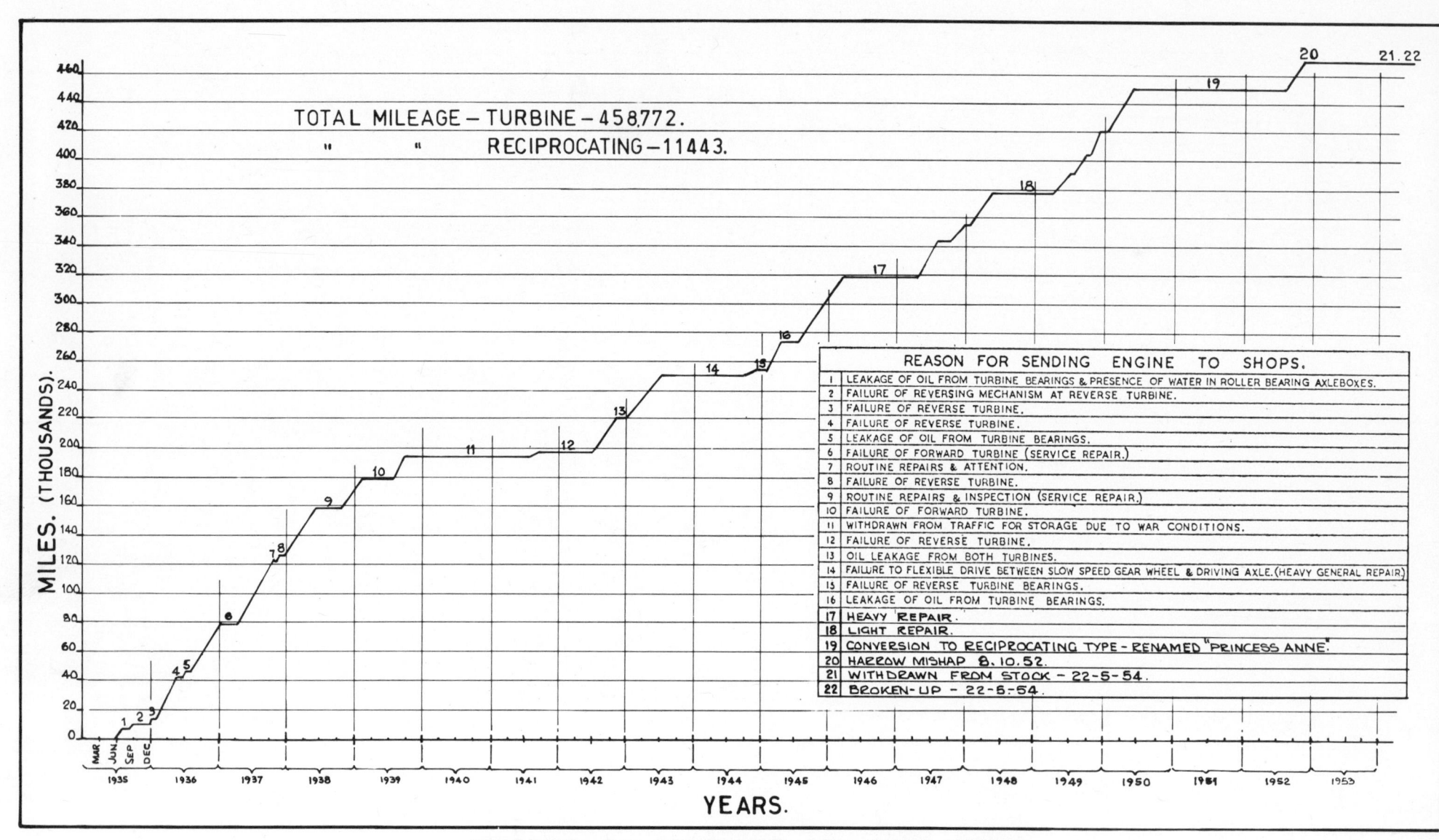

TOTAL MILEAGE — TURBINE — 458,772.
"   "   RECIPROCATING — 11443.

REASON FOR SENDING ENGINE TO SHOPS.	
1	LEAKAGE OF OIL FROM TURBINE BEARINGS & PRESENCE OF WATER IN ROLLER BEARING AXLEBOXES.
2	FAILURE OF REVERSING MECHANISM AT REVERSE TURBINE.
3	FAILURE OF REVERSE TURBINE.
4	FAILURE OF REVERSE TURBINE.
5	LEAKAGE OF OIL FROM TURBINE BEARINGS.
6	FAILURE OF FORWARD TURBINE (SERVICE REPAIR.)
7	ROUTINE REPAIRS & ATTENTION.
8	FAILURE OF REVERSE TURBINE.
9	ROUTINE REPAIRS & INSPECTION (SERVICE REPAIR.)
10	FAILURE OF FORWARD TURBINE.
11	WITHDRAWN FROM TRAFFIC FOR STORAGE DUE TO WAR CONDITIONS.
12	FAILURE OF REVERSE TURBINE.
13	OIL LEAKAGE FROM BOTH TURBINES.
14	FAILURE TO FLEXIBLE DRIVE BETWEEN SLOW SPEED GEAR WHEEL & DRIVING AXLE.(HEAVY GENERAL REPAIR)
15	FAILURE OF REVERSE TURBINE BEARINGS.
16	LEAKAGE OF OIL FROM TURBINE BEARINGS.
17	HEAVY REPAIR.
18	LIGHT REPAIR.
19	CONVERSION TO RECIPROCATING TYPE - RENAMED "PRINCESS ANNE."
20	HARROW MISHAP 8.10.52.
21	WITHDRAWN FROM STOCK - 22-5-54.
22	BROKEN-UP - 22-5-54.

RECORD OF MILEAGE AGAINST TIME.
4-6-2, TURBINE LOCOMOTIVE NO 6202.

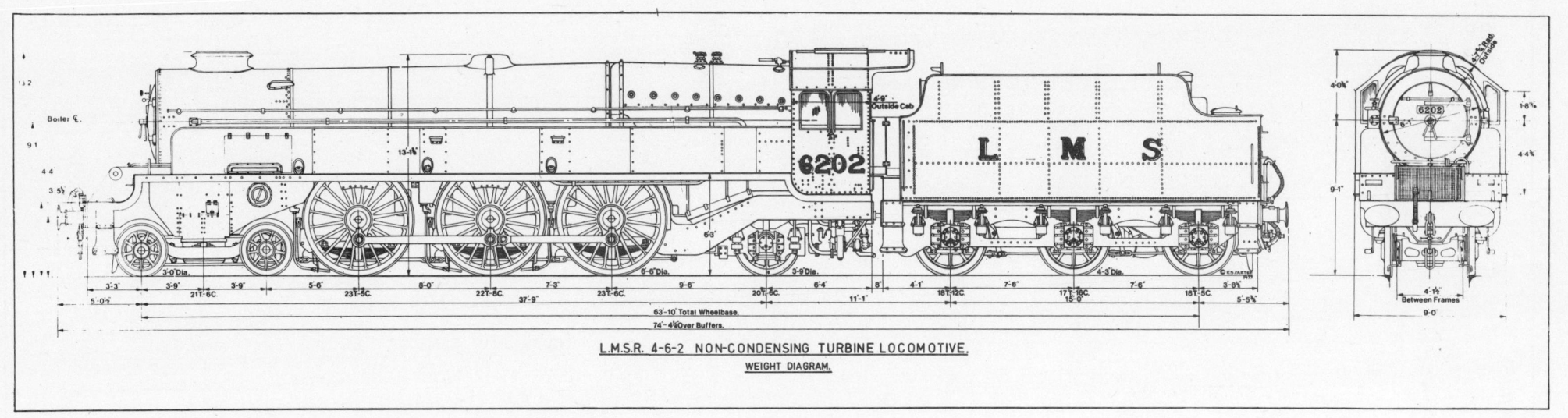

L.M.S.R. 4-6-2 NON-CONDENSING TURBINE LOCOMOTIVE,
WEIGHT DIAGRAM.

COMPARISONS OF STEAM AND ELECTRIC LOCOMOTIVE PERFORMANCE 1935--1978.
AS SHOWN BY A
TABLE OF AVERAGE M.P.H. REGISTERED BETWEEN EUSTON & GLASGOW.
FOR

LOCOMOTIVE TYPE	DATE	LOAD TONS	AV: & MAX: SPEED	ACT: RUN: TIME MIN:	T.E. OR H.P.
TURBOMOTIVE NO: 6202. SHOWN THUS:- ———	6.5.35.	564 TO CREWE. 470 TO SYMINGTON. 331 TO GLASGOW.	53.7 80.0	449	2600 H.P.
STD. CLASS 7 NO: 6212. SHOWN THUS:- -----	11.5.35.	539 TO CREWE 477 TO GLASGOW	52.0 80.0	464	40300 T.E.
CLASS 87 NO. 87001 SHOWN THUS:-— -—--	19.10.78.	339/360 THRO' TO GLASGOW.	83.0 104.0	289.5	5000.H.P.

Graph comparisons overleaf ———>

EUSTON—GLASGOW TIMING CHART

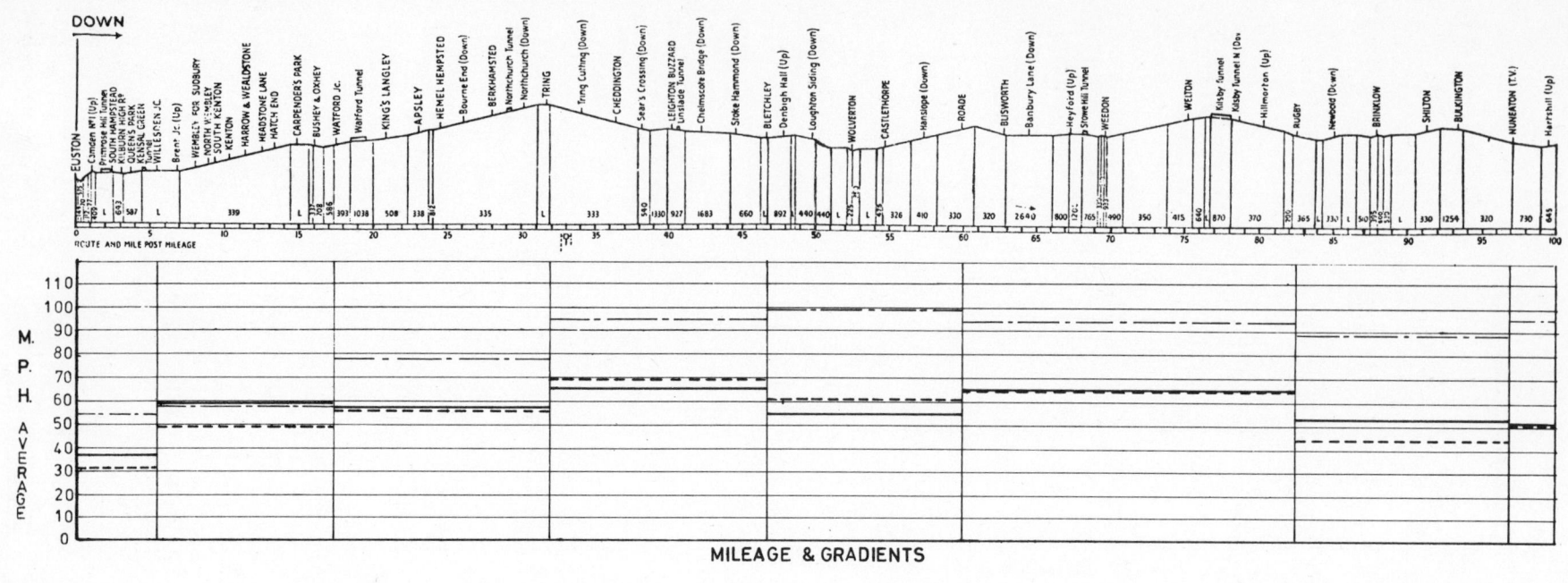

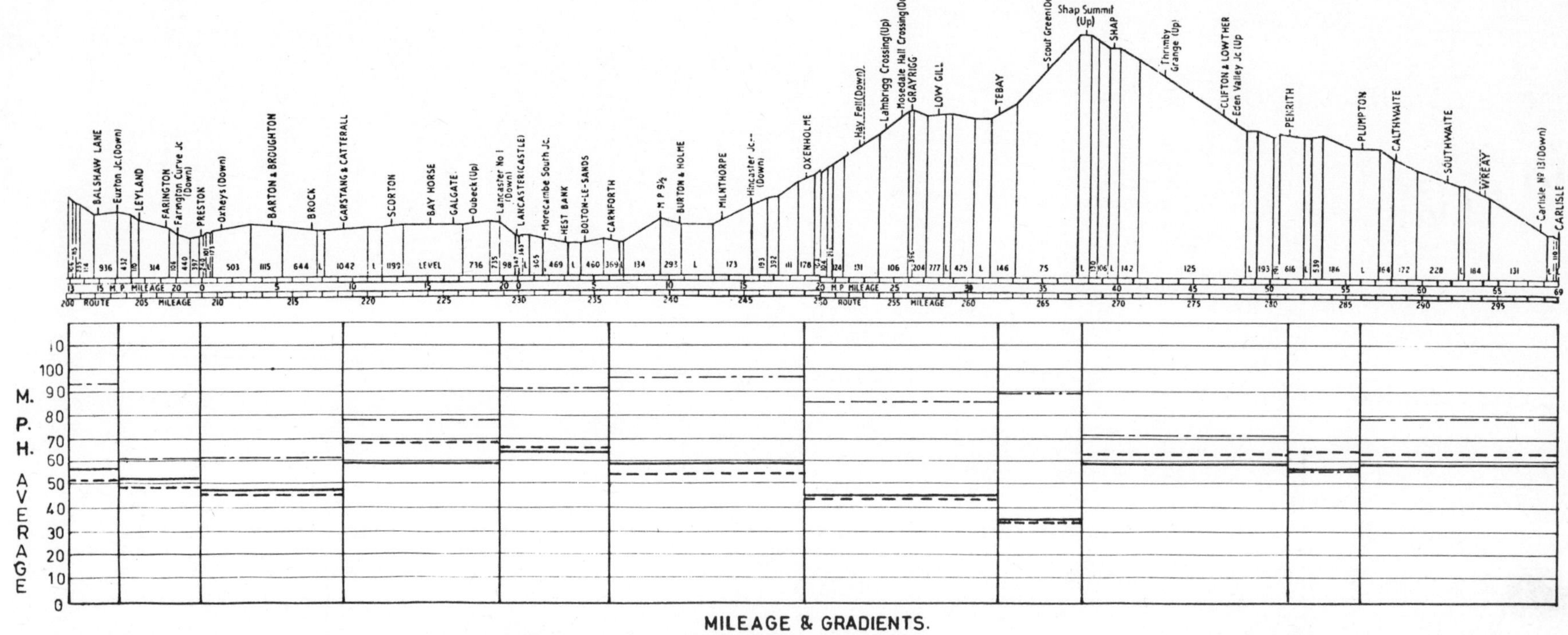

MILEAGE & GRADIENTS

MILEAGE & GRADIENTS.

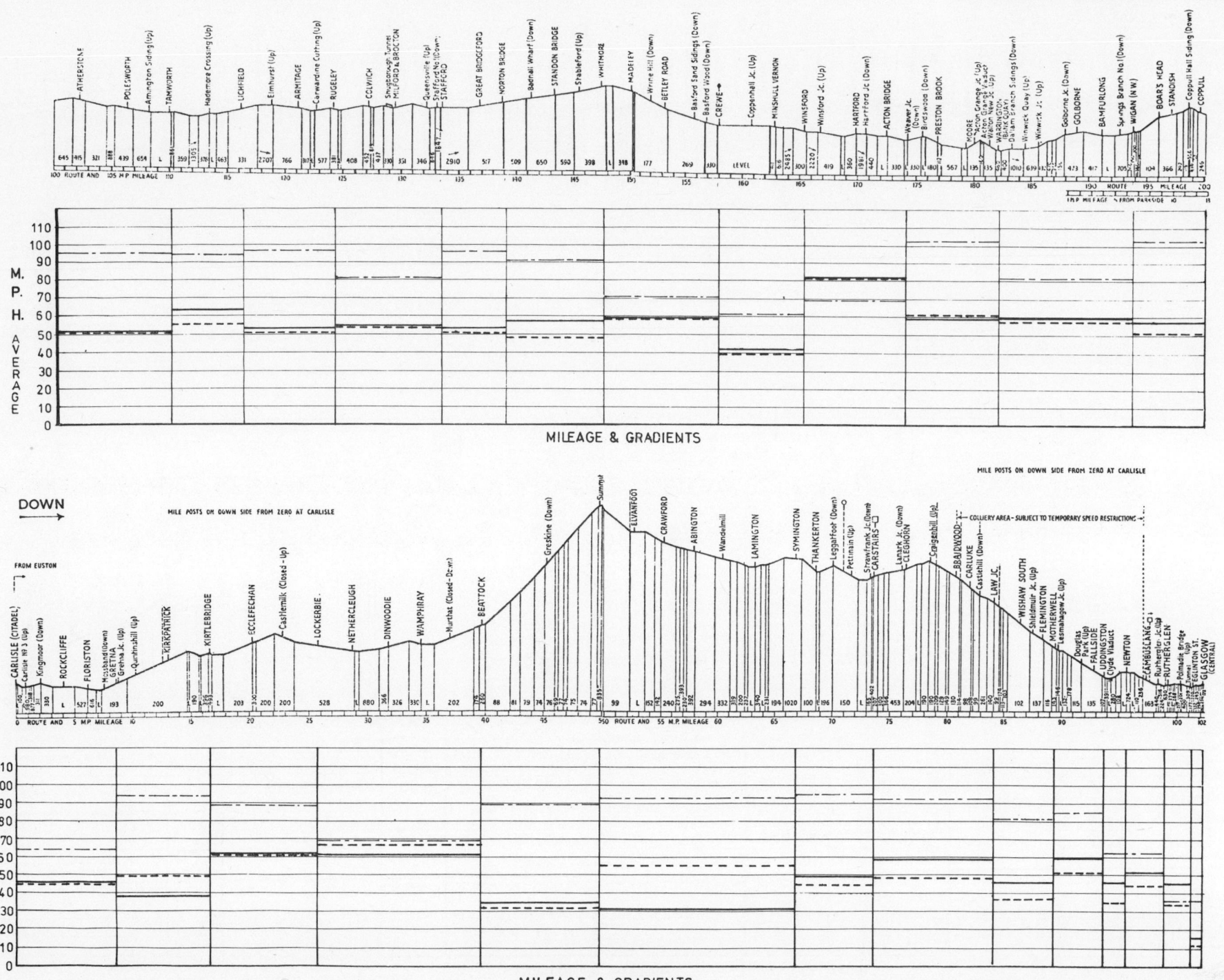

MILEAGE & GRADIENTS

MILEAGE & GRADIENTS.

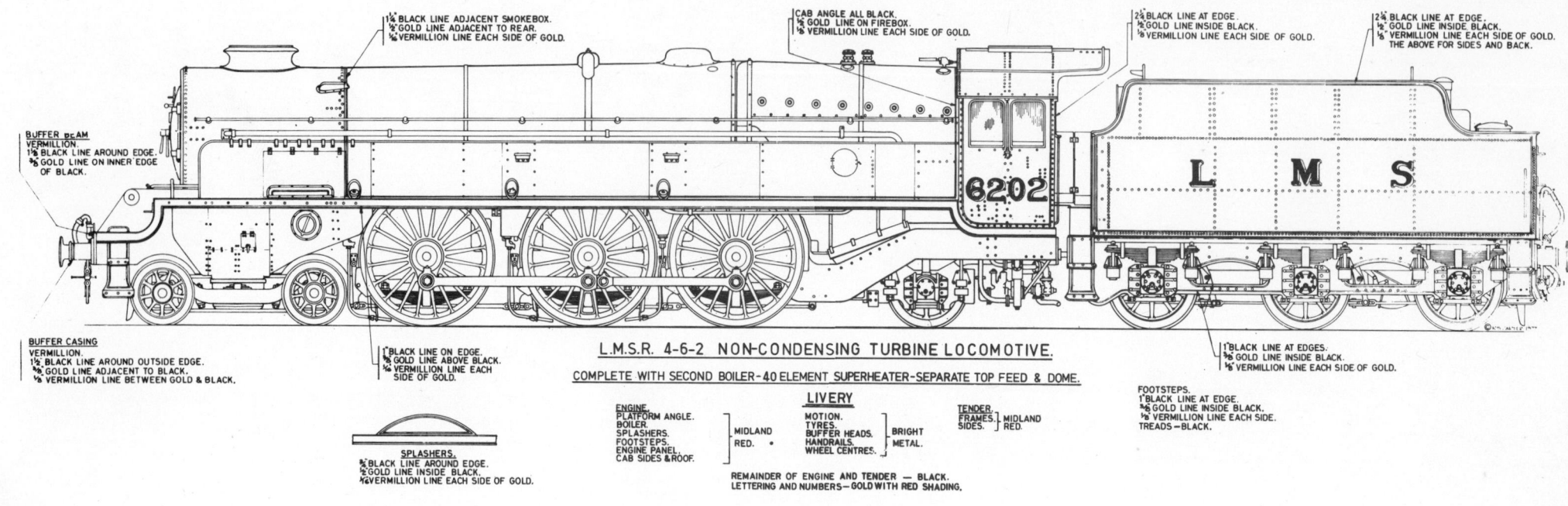

1¼" BLACK LINE ADJACENT SMOKEBOX.
½" GOLD LINE ADJACENT TO REAR.
⅛" VERMILLION LINE EACH SIDE OF GOLD.

CAB ANGLE ALL BLACK.
½" GOLD LINE ON FIREBOX.
⅛" VERMILLION LINE EACH SIDE OF GOLD.

2¼" BLACK LINE AT EDGE.
½" GOLD LINE INSIDE BLACK.
⅛" VERMILLION LINE EACH SIDE OF GOLD.

2¼" BLACK LINE AT EDGE.
½" GOLD LINE INSIDE BLACK.
⅛" VERMILLION LINE EACH SIDE OF GOLD.
THE ABOVE FOR SIDES AND BACK.

BUFFER BEAM
VERMILLION.
1½" BLACK LINE AROUND EDGE.
⅜" GOLD LINE ON INNER EDGE
OF BLACK.

BUFFER CASING
VERMILLION.
1½" BLACK LINE AROUND OUTSIDE EDGE.
⅜" GOLD LINE ADJACENT TO BLACK.
⅛" VERMILLION LINE BETWEEN GOLD & BLACK.

1" BLACK LINE ON EDGE.
½" GOLD LINE ABOVE BLACK.
⅛" VERMILLION LINE EACH
SIDE OF GOLD.

SPLASHERS.
⅜" BLACK LINE AROUND EDGE.
½" GOLD LINE INSIDE BLACK.
⅛" VERMILLION LINE EACH SIDE OF GOLD.

1" BLACK LINE AT EDGES.
⅜" GOLD LINE INSIDE BLACK.
⅛" VERMILLION LINE EACH SIDE OF GOLD.

FOOTSTEPS.
1" BLACK LINE AT EDGE.
⅜" GOLD LINE INSIDE BLACK.
⅛" VERMILLION LINE EACH SIDE.
TREADS—BLACK.

L.M.S.R. 4-6-2 NON-CONDENSING TURBINE LOCOMOTIVE.

COMPLETE WITH SECOND BOILER-40 ELEMENT SUPERHEATER-SEPARATE TOP FEED & DOME.

LIVERY

ENGINE.				
PLATFORM ANGLE.		MOTION.		
BOILER.		TYRES.		
SPLASHERS.	MIDLAND	BUFFER HEADS.	BRIGHT	
FOOTSTEPS.	RED.	HANDRAILS.	METAL.	
ENGINE PANEL.		WHEEL CENTRES.		
CAB SIDES & ROOF.				

TENDER.
FRAMES. } MIDLAND
SIDES. } RED.

REMAINDER OF ENGINE AND TENDER — BLACK.
LETTERING AND NUMBERS—GOLD WITH RED SHADING.

ACKNOWLEDGEMENTS
I would like to thank the following for assistance given in the compilation and
preparation of this book:
The Council of the Institution of Mechanical Engineers—Railway Division
The Editor, Railway Gazette
The National Railway Museum, York
The late Bishop Eric Treacy
Mr. Ian Partridge